IMAGES
of America

ROCKLAND LAKE, HOOK MOUNTAIN, AND NYACK BEACH

IMAGES
of America

ROCKLAND LAKE, HOOK MOUNTAIN, AND NYACK BEACH

Robert C. Maher Jr.

ARCADIA
PUBLISHING

Published by Arcadia Publishing
Charleston, South Carolina

Library of Congress Control Number: 2011940755

For all general information, please contact Arcadia Publishing:
Telephone 843-853-2070
Fax 843-853-0044
E-mail sales@arcadiapublishing.com
For customer service and orders:
Toll-Free 1-888-313-2665

Visit us on the Internet at www.arcadiapublishing.com

This book is dedicated to my mother, Catherine "K" Stevens Maher, who instilled in me the belief that anything is achievable and to all the former residents and future generations who love Rockland Lake.

CONTENTS

ACKNOWLEDGMENTS

It is with deepest gratitude that I thank all the staff at Arcadia Publishing; without the assistance of Rebekah Collinsworth and Caitrin Cunningham, this book would not have been possible. Special thanks go to Jim Hall and Sue Smith of the Palisades Interstate Park Commission (PIPC) for encouraging me to tell the very special history of Rockland Lake, Hook Mountain, and Nyack Beach.

This book would also not have been possible without the assistance of Brian Jennings of the Nyack Library and the Andrew Van Cura collection and of Joanne Potanovic and Marianne B. Leese of the Historical Society of Rockland County. And of course a very special thank-you goes to my friend Robert Knight, historian for the town of Clarkstown, who has contributed so much to so many Arcadia publications on the history of Rockland County.

I finally thank all the former residents of Rockland Lake for sharing their stories of this great area with me. They were truly the inspiration for me to take on this book and share with the community the history of this great area.

INTRODUCTION

Today, we know Rockland Lake, Hook Mountain, and Nyack Beach State Parks as peaceful places to walk, bike, swim, fish, hawk watch, observe nature, and walk a section of the 347-mile Long Path from Fort Lee, New Jersey, to Altamont, New York. Approximately two million people a year visit these parks, ranking them in the top five most-visited state parks in New York, but few have any idea of their rich and vibrant histories.

The Parks of Rockland Lake, Hook Mountain, and Nyack Beach are contiguous land yet make up three different state parks in the town of Clarkstown, 30 miles north of New York City. Hook Mountain is part of the Palisades escarpment that runs along the western shore of the Hudson River from Jersey City, New Jersey, to Haverstraw Bay, New York. Hook Mountain extends eastward into the Tappan Zee section of the Hudson River, causing a bend in the river's north-south orientation. (This section of the Hudson River was named by the Dutch after the local Lanape people who lived along the New Jersey Highlands and northeast to the Hudson Palisades; the Dutch referred to these people as the "Tappan" tribe, and "Zee" means "wide expanse of water.") Hook Mountain's highest point at 728 feet and location along the river's edge prompted the early Dutch sailors to call this mountain Verdriegete Hoek—"the Troublesome Point." The practical Dutch sailors had experienced the unpredictable strength of the gales that sweep around its base and the dead calm waters with no wind blowing only a few feet away. I have sailed beneath the Hook many times always to be fooled by a good wind that just stops; seeing sailboats only a few hundred feet away have a full sail will leave any experienced sailor frustrated.

The Palisades cliffs, including Hook Mountain, were designated a National Natural Landmark in 1980, being the best example of a thick diabase sill in the United States that was formed about 200 to 180 million years ago (late Early Jurassic period). Nyack Beach is located on the southern side of Hook Mountain. Rockland Lake sits on the western slope of the Palisades ridge 168 feet above the Hudson River. The lake is accessible to the river only by a winding break or "clove" in the ridge north of Hook Mountain. Rockland Lake is the only naturally spring-fed lake entirely located in Rockland County. The importance of Rockland Lake goes back to the time of the local Lenni-Lenape tribe who called the lake "Quashpeak." Later, the early European settlers referred to the lake as "the Pond."

The first European settler in the area was John Slaughter. In 1710–1711, he bought a tract of land that included the clove in the mountains where a narrow and precipitous path led from the lake to the river. There, he built a boat landing with commercial traffic growing gradually, but Nyack and Haverstraw, New York, had better natural river facilities. Slaughter's Landing, as the first hamlet was called, was just a small river point of call. In 1884, Rev. David Cole's *History of Rockland County*, one of the first histories written about the county, the origin of the hamlet's name is described as follows: "The landing until quite recent years was called Slaughter's Landing, which name it received from the fact that during the war [American Revolution], the

British foraging parties would land here, scour the county around for cattle, collect them on the beach, where they were slaughtered, and afterwards taken on board the vessels."

It may be true that the British slaughtered cattle at this location; however, no other historical reference regarding this origin for the name of Slaughter's Landing is indicated this way anywhere else.

A significant Revolutionary War event occurred in July 1780, about one mile north of Slaughter's Landing, when Maj. John Andre met with Maj. Gen. Benedict Arnold to hand over plans for the capture of West Point, New York. This location is within Rockland Lake State Park boundaries.

By most accounts, the area started to gain significant historical importance around 1826. It was then that C. Wortendyke of New Jersey came to "the Pond," cut two boatloads of ice, and shipped it to New York City. Most accounts, however, say that the true origin of ice harvesting at Rockland Lake was the work of three men in 1831.

That year, Nathaniel Barmore, John Felter, and Peter Gasque stored about 125 tons of ice underground, then, at the start of the summer, shipped it to New York City by steamboat. In 1836, 20 men each contributed $100 to form a capital fund of $2,000 for the purpose of supplying the city of New York with ice under the name of Barmore, Felter & Company.

With this capital, the company built a new dock at Slaughter's Landing and a small icehouse at the lake that was capable of holding 200 to 300 tons of ice. A cellar on Christopher Street near Greenwich Avenue in New York City was rented to store the ice brought to the city.

Before this time, ice was rare in New York City. It was used primarily by butchers and hotels, rather than in private houses. Most of the ice in the city was supplied with water from wells and cisterns; the ice harvested from the city's neighborhood ponds was too dirty to mix with water for drinking purposes. The purity of Rockland Lake ice made it at once popular. The new Astor House Hotel in New York City, considered one of the finest hotels in the country, contracted ice from Rockland Lake to be ready when its doors opened in 1836. Coincidentally, the hotel was demolished in 1926, the same year that the Rockland Lake icehouses burned to the ground, making the 90-year life of the great hotel concomitant with the glory years of the Rockland Lake ice industry.

As the quality and demand for ice grew, it was determined that the lake's name, "the Pond," was too drab for the source of high-quality ice that brought premium prices, and the name "Rockland Lake" was chosen for the area. It is intriguing to note that, looking to cash in on the reputation of Rockland Lake ice harvesting in New York, a Norwegian ice company renamed one of its harvesting lakes "Rockland Lake" to make the market for Norwegian ice in London more appealing and expensive.

Around the same time the ice industry was starting, rock quarrying along the Palisades had moved north from New Jersey. The quarry operation kept the men employed during the ice harvesting off-season. It was this quarrying operation at Nyack Beach, Hook Mountain, and north of Hook Mountain that gives us the shape of the Palisades cliffs that we see today. Millions of tons of traprock were quarried, crushed, and shipped to New York City for paving streets and constructing the buildings of the fast-growing city.

In 1900, the Palisades Interstate Park Commission (PIPC) was formed to stop the rock quarrying along the New Jersey section of the Palisades. Not until around 1911 would the PIPC be able to stop the quarrying at Nyack Beach and, later, Hook Mountain. The PIPC then established an amusement park along the river that was a favorite stop of paddlewheel steamships, carrying day-trippers from New York City. At the park, visitors could swim in the river, ride a merry-go-round carousel, play games of chance, play baseball, and patronize concession stands. This river park lasted until the 1960s, when the development of the present-day Rockland Lake State Park took shape and opened.

One

NYACK BEACH AND HOOK MOUNTAIN RIVERFRONT

The Palisades, meaning "fence of stakes," were named by the explorers with Giovanni da Verrazano in 1524, as they resembled the log forts built by local Indians. The cliffs, running parallel to the western shoreline of the Hudson River, created the ideal location to easily obtain much needed traprock for the fast-expanding New York City, just 30 miles south. The traprock by its natural characteristics is ideally suited for use as crushed rock for road and housing construction in concrete, macadam, and paving stone. From the mid- to late 1800s, three rock quarry operations were established at Nyack Beach: the Manhattan Traprock Company; Hook Mountain, the Fross and Conklin (also known as Rockland Lake) Traprock Company; and about a mile north, the Haverstraw Traprock Company. In 1900, the Palisades Interstate Park Commission (PIPC) was formed by Govs. Theodore Roosevelt of New York and Foster M. Voorhees of New Jersey in reaction to the damage of the Palisades by quarry operators. By 1911, the PIPC obtained control of the Manhattan Traprock Company and proceeded to acquire both the Fross and Conklin and Haverstraw Traprock Companies. Under the direction of the Civilian Conservation Corps (CCC), the riverfront from Nyack Beach, past Hook Mountain and up to Haverstraw, was transformed into a wonderful riverfront park with stone-lined paths, picnic areas, and ball fields. This all fell into disrepair once the new Rockland Lake State Park was opened in 1965.

Old Rock Mountain Quarry, Hudson River, N.Y.

The Old Rock Mountain Quarry was owned by the Manhattan Traprock Company. The wooden trestle rail dock extended into the Hudson River so that barges could load up on the traprock for shipment to New York City. Note the powerhouse in the lower left of picture and the two tunnels in the mountain face. This picture was taken in the early 1900s. (Courtesy of the PIPC Archives.)

The Old Rock Mountain Quarry, looking north from the Hudson River, is pictured here. Note the extensive damage to the Palisades cliffs caused by the rock quarry industry. There are piles of lose stone and man-made mountain plateaus. (Courtesy of the PIPC Archives.)

Pictured is the Manhattan Traprock Company's wooden trestle rail dock; in 1911, the company was purchased by the PIPC for $425,000. The powerhouse to the left is still standing, and the tunnels in the hillside remain today but are covered by tree growth. This picture was taken in June 1926. (Courtesy of the PIPC Archives.)

This June 1926 photograph shows the powerhouse of the Manhattan Traprock Company gutted of all its old equipment. The structure was made of poured-in-place concrete. The PIPC received funding for the purchase and construction of the new Nyack Beach Park from the Rockefeller Foundation, Mary W. Harriman, J.P. Morgan, and others. (Courtesy of the PIPC Archives.)

Pictured is the Manhattan Traprock Company powerhouse building. Note the large chimney and the concrete cap on top as well as the roofline. This June 1926 picture was taken just before renovations were started on the building for park use. (Courtesy of the PIPC Archives.)

The Manhattan Traprock Company powerhouse building was converted into the Nyack–Hook Mountain Beach bathhouse by the Civilian Conservation Corps (CCC). Workers covered the concrete building with local stone and constructed a cafeteria inside a main hall with a second-floor gallery to view the Hudson River. The front covered porch has since been removed, but the large chimney concrete cap is still visible just above the roof line. (Courtesy of the PIPC Archives.)

Rockland Lake Traprock Company was owned by Foss and Conklin. This picture is looking south with Hook Mountain on the right. (Author's collection.)

Seen in 1916 is the Rockland Lake Traprock Company stone crusher building. This image is looking from the Hudson River with Hook Mountain in the background. Note the barges in the Hudson River ready to transport stone to New York City. The Rockland Lake Landing is to the right of the picture. (Courtesy of the PIPC Archives.)

This photograph of Hook Mountain rock quarry operations shows a rail tracks that will transport the stone to the Rockland Lake Traprock stone crusher. A total of six rail carts can be seen at the bottom of the picture. (Author's collection.)

Pictured is the Hook Mountain rock quarry operation. This image clearly represents the meaning of the Palisades cliffs—"fence of stakes"— as named by the explorers with Verrazano in 1524 since they resembled the log forts built by the local Indians. (Author's collection.)

15

The site of the Rockland Lake Traprock Company, looking south at Hook Mountain, shows the destruction of the mountain over the years. This picture was taken in June 1926. (Courtesy of the PIPC Archives.)

Looking north at Hook Mountain in June 1926, one can see the destruction done by the rock quarry operation. (Courtesy of the PIPC Archives.)

Hook Mountain is in the center of the picture with the Rockland Lake Traprock stone crusher at the far-left side and, at the right, the Rockland Lake ice chute and landing going up the mountain cove into the town of Rockland Lake. (Author's collection.)

Hook mountain - from pier - Rockland, n.y.

This 1906 picture, looking south at Hook Mountain, shows Henry Vorrath's Hudson River Hotel, one of the first hotels in Rockland Lake, at center. It was often used by people sailing on the Hudson River who did not want to travel to the town of Rockland Lake, which sits about 200 feet above the Hudson River. (Courtesy of the PIPC Archives.)

In this 1914 view is the Haverstraw Rock Quarry located north of Rockland Lake Landing at Hook Mountain. The row of round concrete structures going up the hill is still present today along the park trail. (Courtesy of the PIPC Archives.)

The dismantling of the Rockland Lake Traprock stone crushers is pictured here. Note the workmen near the bottom of the beams. This structure was at least five stories tall and framed out of steel. Steel construction was a very new method for building in the early 1900s. (Collection of Andrew Van Cura.)

Hudson River from the Mountain, showing Light House, Rockland Lake, N. Y.

The rock quarry workmen's shed is seen on top of Hook Mountain, and the Rockland Lake Lighthouse is visible in the Hudson River. The rock formation in this picture is a good example of the Palisades Sill, which was formed from solidified magma during the Triassic period. (Author's collection.)

19

From the middle of the river, the Rockland Lake Lighthouse marked the Rockland Lake Landing. Hook Mountain and the Foss and Conklin stone crusher are by the river's edge, at the left. Workers' homes are going up the hill behind the lighthouse, into the town of Rockland Lake. (Author's collection.)

Rockland Lake Lighthouse is seen in the winter with a frozen Hudson River. It was not uncommon for the Hudson River to freeze. Once, the author's grandfather Theodore Stevens ice-skated across the river to Ossining, New York, to purchase salt for preserving food, as the town of Rockland Lake was snowbound and out of supplies. (Author's collection.)

The *Chrystenah* paddlewheel steamboat and its sister ship, the *Clinton*, were contracted by the Palisades Interstate Park Commission to bring day-trippers from New York City, departing from West Tenth and Twenty-second Streets to the Hudson River parks, including Nyack Beach, Hook Mountain, Rockland Lake, and Bear Mountain farther north. In later years, the PIPC purchased two ferries, the *Bear Mountain* and *Alexander Hamilton*, due to increased park use. (Author's collection.)

This steamboat is thought to be the *Clinton* passing along the Palisades cliffs that run from Jersey City, New Jersey, north to Haverstraw, New York. Behind the boat, one can see stone rubble left from the old quarry operations. (Author's collection.)

Chrystenah arriving at Rockland Lake, N. Y.

The steamboat *Chrystenah* is pushed into docking position by a river tugboat. The Rockland Lake Lighthouse Landing is to the left of the bow of the ship. (Author's collection.)

The steamboat *Chrystenah* is docked at the Rockland Lake Landing. This is the same dock that was used for ice shipments from the icehouses at Rockland Lake to New York City. This dock is located just north of the Hook Mountain Park Landing. (Author's collection.)

As many as two to three steamships from New York City would tie up together to disembark passengers for their day trips. The carrousel building is in the background. (Courtesy of the PIPC Archives.)

BATHhouse and Beach
Hook Mountain Park N.Y.

204

At the Hook Mountain Park boat landing, the building in the foreground on the right was a 36-by-72-foot bathhouse, complete with showers and lockers, so bathers could enjoy a swim in the Hudson River. (Courtesy of the PIPC Archives.)

Hook Mountain Park cafeteria is seen around 1929. Today, the wood components of the building are gone, but the stone piers and foundation still exist. (Courtesy of the PIPC Archives.)

Hook Mountain Park boat landing is seen from the shore. The buildings in the foreground were comfort stations that were basic outhouse engineering. (Courtesy of the PIPC Archives.)

The Hook Mountain Park carousel building was but one of the many amusements along the waterfront where one could catch the river breeze on a hot summer day. Note the close location to the river's edge. It was during a storm that this building was destroyed. The concrete footings can still be found today. (Courtesy of the PIPC Archives.)

Hook Mountain Park was full of entertainment; this is the dance pavilion. It was 92 feet in diameter and located along the river's edge. This picture is from the 1940s. (Courtesy of the PIPC Archives.)

Two

ICE INDUSTRY

As the demand for ice grew during the 1830s and 1840s, so did the number of companies forming ice-harvesting businesses at Rockland Lake, causing fierce competition. In 1855, three of the competing companies, acknowledging their common interest and need, incorporated as the Knickerbocker Ice Company. This successful consolidation and the continuing growth of the ice trade prompted a major investment in the facilities at Rockland Lake. In 1860, work was completed on an inclined railway from the Hudson River up through the clove of the Palisades ridge and into the town of Rockland Lake, which sits about 200 feet above the river, and then down to Rockland Lake, which lies 160 feet above the river. Of all the advances and accomplishments of the Knickerbocker Ice Company, it was the inclined railway that attracted the greatest attention. To celebrate its completion, a champagne reception was held on September 25, 1860, to which the *Rockland County Journal* reported the following:

> Now we never drank a glass of iced champagne in our whole lifetime, and so long as we retain our senses we never intend to; so it was not that which took us to the Lake. But they have been doing a great work there; something that speaks well for Rockland County in general, and the KNICKERBOCKER ICE CO., in particular. They have constructed a monument, in which scientific and mechanical skill, liberal enterprise, nice ingenuity, and even a dash of witty genius, are all combined. Out of a little iron and wood and wire, has grown up a beautiful, symmetrical and imposing structure, honorable to its projectors and one more attestation to the useful inventive genius of our countrymen.

So impressive was the inclined railway and the ice works that Thomas Edison visited in 1898 and again, in 1902, to take film footage of the ice-harvesting operation that can still be seen today.

This is a view from the lake toward the center of town. The main icehouse's power plant is in the foreground with the tall chimney. Toward the top of the chimney is the Continental Hotel, and to the left of that is the Methodist church. On the upper right side of the photograph is the original school building. (Author's collection.)

Filling Middle House, Rockland Lake, N. Y.

Through a channel of ice, the men would push the ice blocks to each elevator located on the side of the icehouse. Note that the horizontal supports are actually paths used to bring the ice up to each level of the icehouse. This building would have been about four stories tall. (Author's collection.)

No. 29. Harvesting Ice from Rockland Lake, N. Y. "Cutting".

Published by Chas. Walter. Made in Germany.

Men, horses, ice plows, and ice saws were important tools for the harvesting of ice from Rockland Lake. The day would begin at 4:30 a.m. with the feeding of the horses and go until 6:00 p.m. This required standing out on the cold, windy lake for more than 12 hours a day. (Author's collection.)

This group photograph is of nine ice fishers, or ice harvesters, as they were called. The winter protection typically consisted of wool clothing and leather boots. It would keep the men warm when they were dry, but since the men often had to stand on the ice all day, their clothing would get wet, leaving the men vulnerable to sickness. (Collection of Andrew Van Cura.)

Knickerbocker Icehouse No. 1 is pictured in the mid-1800s. There were many icehouses around the northeast side of the lake. (Author's collection.)

BIRD'S EYE VIEW OF ICE HOUSES, ROCKLAND LAKE, N. Y.

After the closure of the Knickerbocker Ice Company, New York State senator Ellwood Rabenold purchased the lake and much of the land from the former ice company. On April 20, 1926, workmen were dismantling one of the icehouses when a grass fire started, burning an icehouse storing dynamite. The explosion sent logs and fire embers across the town; 10 homes caught fire and burned. The fire also put the lodge of James W. Gerard, former ambassador to Germany, at risk. (Collection of Andrew Van Cura.)

This is one of the larger icehouses on the lake. The icehouse was painted white to keep it cooler in the summer months. The ice ramps have eight horizontal levels; these horizontal sections not only added strength to the building but also allowed ice blocks to be taken to and stored at each level of the icehouse. (Author's collection.)

This is a close-up view of an ice ramp. Each rung on the ramp held a block of ice as it moved into the icehouse to be stored. Note the height of the icehouse compared to the two-story house to the right of the ramp. (Collection of Andrew Van Cura.)

Pictured is a drawing of an icehouse being loaded. The blocks of ice would come up from the lake on the elevator and down a ramp to be sent into the different rooms within the icehouse. (Author's collection.)

This drawing is of the outside of an icehouse. When filling an icehouse, each block of ice was placed at a right angle to the layer below it, and a space was left between the blocks of ice so that the blocks of ice did not freeze together. (Author's collection.)

Men are sending ice blocks to the icehouses. Note the large house on the top of the hill in the center of picture. This house belonged to one of the owners of Knickerbocker Ice Company, the Wells family. A family cemetery is still located on the top of the mountain. (Author's collection.)

BIRD'S EYE VIEW OF TOWN, ROCKLAND LAKE, N. Y.

This picture was taken looking from the top of an icehouse ramp toward the town. The building on the right behind the white building is the steam house that ran all the cables and ropes for the ice elevators. This picture is where parking lot No. 2 is currently located at Rockland Lake State Park. (Collection of Robert Knight.)

This is a bird's-eye view of town and the ice power plant. Based on the angle of the photograph, it is most likely that the photograph was taken on the roof of the icehouses that would have stood where present-day Rockland Lake State Park parking lot No. 2 is located. (Author's collection.)

ICE HOUSE, Rockland Lake, N. Y.   Hand Colored

The icehouse on the left was the largest; it was 200 feet wide by 500 feet long and five stories tall. (Author's collection.)

Rockland Lake, N. Y.

This picture was taken from the west side of Rockland Lake. Left of the center is the powerhouse, above that is the Continental Hotel, and off to the left is the bell tower of the Methodist church. (Author's collection.)

Once the ice carts were mechanically lifted up the hill from the lake to the center of town, horses would tow the wagons through town on tracks over to the top of the ice chute that led down toward the Hudson River landing dock. (Collection of Nyack Library.)

This half-gauge steam engine traveled between the icehouses to bring the ice carts to the lake powerhouse that then transported the ice carts up the hill to the center of town. (Collection of Nyack Library.)

This picture was taken from Rockland Lake Road at the intersection of Main Street. It shows the powerhouse to the left. The ice was brought up the hill on carts pulled by chains to the top of the hill and into the center of town. (Collection of Robert Knight.)

This wintertime picture was taken from Rockland Lake Road at the intersection of Main Street. From the lake to the center of town, the ice carts would have to go up hill about 40 feet in elevation. (Collection of Robert Knight.)

This is one of the few known pictures of the ice chute mechanical house on the top of the hill leading down toward the river. The ice carts would enter on the right of the building and exit to go down 200 feet in elevation on the left side of the building. (Courtesy of the PIPC Archives.)

This view is from the top of the ice chute. The chute traveled down to the Hudson River where ice barges waited to be loaded for shipment to New York City. (Collection of Robert Knight.)

INCLINE R. R. AND ICE SLIDE, LAKE LANDING, ROCKLAND LAKE, N. Y.

Pictured is the Rockland Lake ice chute. The building on the right of the chute is Henry Vorrath's Hudson River Hotel. It was said that, as the ice came down the ramp, it sounded like a freight train was coming through the hotel. (Collection of Robert Knight.)

This picture was taken from the end of the pier in the Hudson River, looking back up the hill toward the town of Rockland Lake. The ice carts worked on a gravity system. Carts loaded with ice coming down the mountain would pull empty carts back to the top. Hook Mountain is to the left. (Author's collection.)

The Rockland Lake ice chute is shown in this winter picture. Note the two sets of tracks; they were used to move the ice carts onto the barges. The ice chute starts about 200 feet above the Hudson River. The ice carts came down the hill at great speeds and were attached to cables to be used as braking. (Courtesy of the PIPC Archives.)

A-1574. Foot of Mountain, Rockland Lake, N. Y.

Landing Road, pictured here, goes down to Hudson River's edge. The ice chute is just past the white house in the center. Hook Mountain is the hillside to the right of the picture. (Collection of Robert Knight.)

Henry Vorrath's Hudson River Hotel was constructed prior to the ice chute that passed on the left side of the building. This was a main hotel for River travelers, as they would not need to make the walk up the very steep Landing Road into town to the other hotels. The man standing at the far right with a hat is reported to be Count Alfred Seigling. (Author's collection.)

This Knickerbocker Ice receipt is from 1891. Note the writing at the top reads as follows: "The only Company Bringing Rockland Lake Ice to this Market." At this time, the Knickerbocker Ice Company operated 15 depots throughout the New York City area. (Author's collection.)

This coupon was good for 25 pounds of ice. These coupon books were purchased in advance and given to the iceman upon delivery. This was most likely used in New York City. (Author's collection.)

Three

TOWN OF ROCKLAND LAKE

Rockland Lake with its crystal clear spring-fed waters and the hillside of the Palisades offered an abundance of work and entertainment. From the traprock quarry and ice operations to the enjoyment of swimming, boating, and fishing in the Hudson River or the lake, the town of Rockland Lake drew people from all over the world. The *Rockland County Journal* reprinted in 1863 a French newspaper article written by M. "Sam" Berthollet; Berthollet described the area and people of Rockland Lake as follows:

> The population of this part of North America, though made up of men of all countries, is not recruited as easily as one might suppose. At such an altitude, one does not expose oneself with impunity to such rigorous, cold, and, above all, to such rarefaction of atmosphere. Consequently the ice fishers, such themselves, remind one, by their stunted appearance, of the Laplanders. The race of these men devoted to a deadly profession is constantly wasting away. But as they earn large wages, they lead a life of perils that is not without its charms, and for which they come to have a passionate love; they prefer the summit of Rockland Lake, and its eternal ice, to the life of towns. They are satisfied with drinking gin at discretion, and with the possession of a savage comfort adapted to their gross tastes.

Now, the residents of Rockland Lake were by no means stunted. Though working on the ice and blasting rock in the quarries did have their perils, the town was still full of life. However, by the 1920s, with the closure of the rock quarries and ice industry, the town's main sources of income had all but disappeared. In 1958, former New York State senator Ellwood Rabenold sold the lake and 225 acres of surrounding land to the Palisades Interstate Park Commission. During that summer, many other Rockland Lake landowners also started selling their property to the PIPC. To this day, it is a misunderstanding that the state was going to take the residential land by condemnation. That did occur with some of the rock quarries but was never suggested by the commission for private residents. Some residents did not sell, and today, there are a handful of privately owned homes still located inside the boundaries of Rockland Lake State Park.

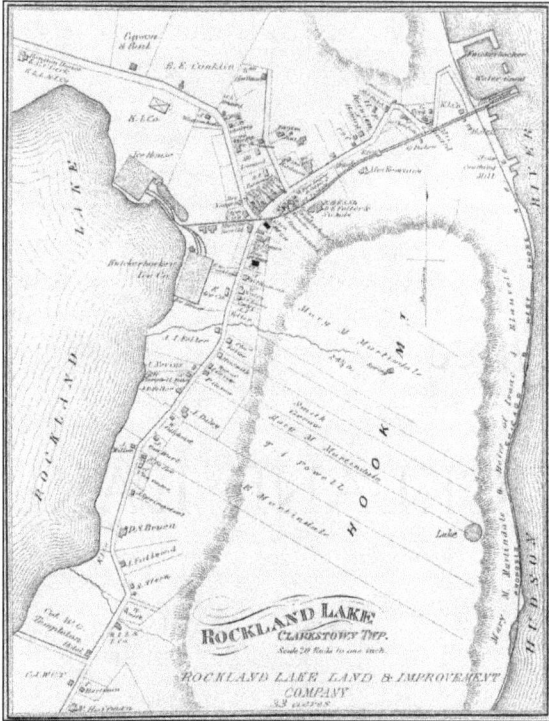

This 1876 map shows the town of Rockland Lake; note the two icehouses by the lake and the path the ice tracks traveled over the mountain, through the town, and down to the Hudson River. Along the shoreline of the Hudson River was the proposed path for the West Shore train line. This route was abandoned due to the rock quarry operation and rerouted into the newly formed town of Congers. (Author's collection.)

The photograph shows many of the main town's important buildings. In the center of the photograph is the Continental Hotel, to the left is the Methodist church, and to the right of the Hotel is the old public school building. In the foreground on the right is the power plant that supplied the mechanical belts to bring the blocks of ice up to the different levels of the icehouses. The powerhouse also supplied the power to bring the ice wagons from the icehouses up the hill to be taken down to the river for shipment. (Author's collection.)

This picture was taken from Collyer Lane (often referred to as "the lane"). There are two large icehouses on the lakeshore on the right of the photograph and the Methodist church with the white bell tower is on the left. (Collection of Nyack Library.)

This is a 1960 aerial view of Collyer Lane. The Hudson River at the top of the image, and the lake is at the bottom left. Some houses were already removed in this picture; today, there are only four houses still occupied in this area. (Courtesy of the PIPC Archives.)

49

New York state senator Abraham B. Congers donated property to the West Shore train line in an effort to increase his property development. Note the sign on the station that reads, "Congers and Rockland Lake, Buffalo 387 miles, NYC 34.5 miles." (Author's collection.)

A horse-drawn coach was used to bring Rockland Lake residents to the train station in Congers. Later, the train station had a spur rail track from Congers to Sylvan Grove at Rockland Lake (today the location of the nature center) to serve the residents and to bring ice to the railcars that traveled the West Shore rail line. (Author's collection.)

Store Hill, also known as Lake Road, is the main road leading into town from the north side of the lake. The picture is looking west from Main Street. In the 1920s, this road became part of US 9W. Many of the stone walls on the right of the picture can still be seen today on Lake Road. (Author's collection.)

The post office was located on the corner of Lake Road and Main Street of Rockland Lake. The post office closed in 1965. The town consolidated into a neighboring town. The last postmistress was Florence Brinkerhoff. (Courtesy of the PIPC Archives.)

Rockland Lake's Main Street is shown in the 1900s. The picture was taken from the corner of Main Street and Collyer Lane. The town consisted of two butcher shops, a general store, a post office, and a long-standing candy shop. (Author's collection.)

MAIN STREET, Rockland Lake, N. Y.

Pictured is Main Street in Rockland Lake. The Continental Hotel is in the center of the picture, and the Methodist church is the tall bell tower on the left. (Author's collection.)

Michael Ladik's Department Store, Rockland Lake, N.

The late-1800s corner of Collyer Lane and Main Street was home to Ladik's Department Store. The store was known as the place in town to get everything people needed, from food and clothing to farm equipment. (Courtesy of the PIPC Archives.)

Local men and a dog relax on the steps of a store in the early 1900s. The man with the white shirt is holding a meat-hanging hook. (Collection of Nyack Library.)

Rockland Lake's Main Street is shown in the 1960s, at the corner of Main Street and Collyer Lane. This picture was taken by the PIPC, as it made plans to purchase the buildings for a park. (Courtesy of the PIPC Archives.)

By the 1960s, the town of Rockland Lake was falling into disrepair. The Continental Hotel, once one of the town's best hotels, was now more than 100 years old and had become a low-income boardinghouse. New owners purchased the hotel in the 1980s and restored it to its once former grandeur. (Courtesy of the PIPC Archives.)

The Continental Hotel was one of many hotels in the town of Rockland Lake. Located at the corner of Main Street and Lake Road, this building still stands today. (Author's collection.)

By the 1970s, the former grandeur of the Continental Hotel had passed, and the building was in great disrepair. It was being used as a single-room occupancy residence. (Courtesy of the PIPC Archives.)

This 1900s picture is of Main Street, looking east from the intersection with Lake Road. Lappe General Store is on the left. The ice wagons coming from the lake would travel from the left to right in this picture. (Author's collection.)

J. W. Lappe General Store 374
Rockland Lake, N. Y.

Lappe General Store in seen in the 1920s; it was one of many stores that supplied the town with goods, including gas. Note the gas pump on the corner. (Collection of Robert Knight.)

Here is Main Street, looking east. This early-1960s picture was taken by the PIPC, as the commission was making offers to purchase the buildings. One can see that, by the 1960s, the town had fallen onto hard times. (Courtesy of the PIPC Archives.)

By the early 1960s, the PIPC had purchased many of the buildings in the town. This picture is of the intersection of Lake Road and Main Street, looking east. Lappe General Store stood on the corner. (Courtesy of the PIPC Archives.)

A-1576. Street Scene, Rockland Lake, N. Y.

Here is Main Street in the 1900s, looking east. On the center right is the path for the ice wagons that leads from the lake and goes behind the town buildings. On the right, behind the picket fence, is the Methodist church. (Collection of Robert Knight.)

The Methodist church stood at the head of the intersection of Main Street and Lake Road. This 1900s photograph shows the ice wagon ramp just to the left of the church's picket fence. (Archives of the Rockland County Historical Society.)

The inside of the Methodist church is decorated with bunting for a special occasion. (Archives of the Rockland County Historical Society.)

This 1900s picture, taken from the hill behind the Methodist church on the left, shows a number of icehouses on the north edge of Rockland Lake. These were small icehouses compared to the icehouses on the east side of the lake. The icehouses pictured here are located where present-day Rockland Lake parking lot No. 2 is found. (Collection of Robert Knight.)

MAIN STREET, Rockland Lake, N. Y.

Here is Main Street in the 1900s, looking east. The public school is on the right. (Collection of Robert Knight.)

The old public grade school with its two entrances, one for boys and one for girls, was destroyed in a fire in the 1920s. (Collection of Robert Knight.)

PUBLIC SCHOOL, Rockland Lake, N. Y.

The new public school building is pictured in the late 1920s. This was an elementary school, housing the first through eighth grades in a typical one-room schoolhouse. After this school, students then attended high school in the neighboring town of Congers. This building still exists today. (Author's collection.)

COMMENCEMENT EXERCISES

ROCKLAND LAKE PUBLIC SCHOOL

WEDNESDAY EVENING

JUNE 28, 1911

AT EIGHT O'CLOCK

Here is the June 28, 1911, graduation program of the author's great-aunt Julia Stevens. The school motto was "Strive and Succeed" (Author's collection.)

St. Michael's Church was a mission church out of Haverstraw. The church building is said to have been originally constructed in Nyack, located on the other side of Hook Mountain, and carried over the mountain for the parishioners of Rockland Lake. It was destroyed by fire in the 1920s. (Author's collection.)

This picture is of those enrolled at St. Michael's School in 1914. The picture shows more than 90 students with two nuns as teachers. (Collection of Andrew Van Cura.)

Pictured in the 1950s, this church replaced the original St. Michael's Church in the 1920s. The parish sold the church to the Palisades Interstate Commission, which demolished the building in the late 1960s. The building to the right is Tillims fabric store. (Courtesy of the PIPC Archives.)

The entrance to St. Michael's Church was not on the street side. The foundation of the tower can still be found today. As the townspeople sold their homes and moved out of town, the church congregation dwindled, and the church could no longer be supported. St. Michael's Church had a cemetery in the town of Rockland Lake that was planned and laid out by the author's great-grandfather Joseph Stevens. This cemetery is still in use today by St. Paul's Church in Congers, New York. (Collection of Andrew Van Cura.)

These houses were for the ice and quarry workmen and their families. They were located behind St. Michael's Church. The PIPC removed them during the 1920s as the commission created Hook Mountain State Park. Note each building contained four to eight families and all shared common outhouses and wells for drinking water. (Courtesy of the PIPC Archives.)

This typical four-family house for workers sat just on the hillside of Hook Mountain with the Hudson River to the left. The ice chute would have run behind the house. (Courtesy of the PIPC Archives.)

This four-family house for workers sat at the bottom of the ice chute. Note the chute is to the right of the house. This picture was taken on March 31, 1926. (Courtesy of the PIPC Archives.)

The town of Rockland Lake supported all levels of society from the working class to the owners of the rock quarries and icehouses. This is an example of one of the finer homes that was located on Main Street. (Courtesy of the PIPC Archives.)

This home was well taken care of when the owners sold it to the PIPC. It is a grand home with a porte cochere on the side. (Courtesy of the PIPC Archives.)

Since the Hudson family lived there, this house is referred to as "the Hudson house." It is still standing but is in great disrepair; it has not been lived in for more than a decade. The house style is Second Empire and was considered an upper- to middle-income home. One-story mansard homes are considered rare examples of Second Empire as the style was often reserved for much larger homes. (Courtesy of the PIPC Archives.)

Josephine Walters Hudson is pictured in the center with her supervisor and one of the many horses she would take care of on the lake. Josephine is the daughter of Charles B. Walters, who is credited with taking the photographs used for many postcards of Rockland Lake. At the age of 13, Josephine, after the death of her mother, wanted to help her family financially. She applied for a job at the ice company and was told no girls were allowed to work the ice fields. The next day, she put her hair up under her hat and got a job as Jo Hudson. She worked with the ice company for a number of years, taking care of the horses. Josephine is thought to be the only female to have worked the ice harvest. She later married into the Hudson family and lived until 1993. Her Hudson family house is pictured on the previous page; it did not have central heat or running water. Josephine was often seen chopping her own firewood well into her nineties. (Collection of Nyack Library.)

This grand home on the hill overlooking the town and river was the home of the Wells family; the Wells were part owners in the Knickerbocker Ice Company and one of the rock quarries. This Victorian home had a widow's walk (an observation deck on the roof). This top of this home is identifiable in many of the pictures of town. (Courtesy of the PIPC Archives.)

This is another example of a fine home that was located on the south end of the lake. This picture was taken in the 1960s by the PIPC. As lovely a home as this was, it, along with many others in town, still did not have indoor plumbing or modern heating systems when the PIPC purchased it. (Courtesy of the PIPC Archives.)

This 1960s picture is of the Knickerbocker Engine Company No.1, established in 1861 by the Knickerbocker Ice Company to protect the company's buildings. The Knickerbocker Engine Company is still active today. (Courtesy of the PIPC Archives.)

The Knickerbocker Fire Engine Company

The Knickerbocker Engine Company is photographed with its 1937 LaFrance fire truck. (Author's collection.)

The Knickerbocker Ice Company baseball team is pictured in the 1900s. Baseball was an outlet from the hard work in the ice business. (Archives of the Rockland County Historical Society.)

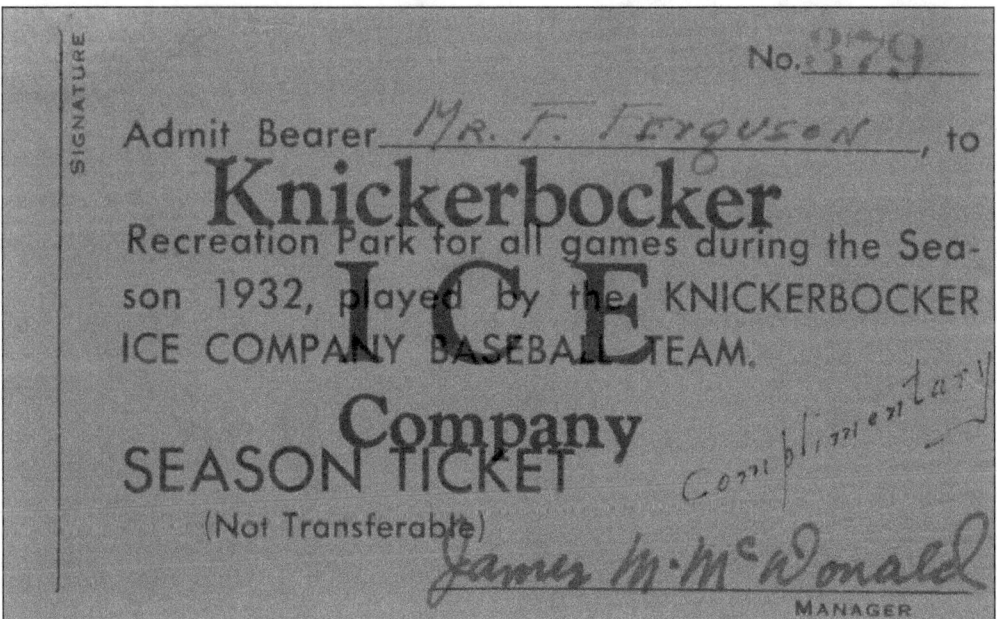

This Knickerbocker Ice Company 1932 baseball season ticket belonged to Mr. F. Ferguson. (Author's collection.)

The author's home is shown in 1960; at that time, the PIPC was making an offer to purchase it from the author's grandmother Frances Stevens. She did not sell, and the property has now been in the family for move than 170 years. The house was originally a two-family ice workers' home and was moved by the author's great-grandfather Joseph Stevens by horse and wagon to its current location. (Courtesy of the PIPC Archives.)

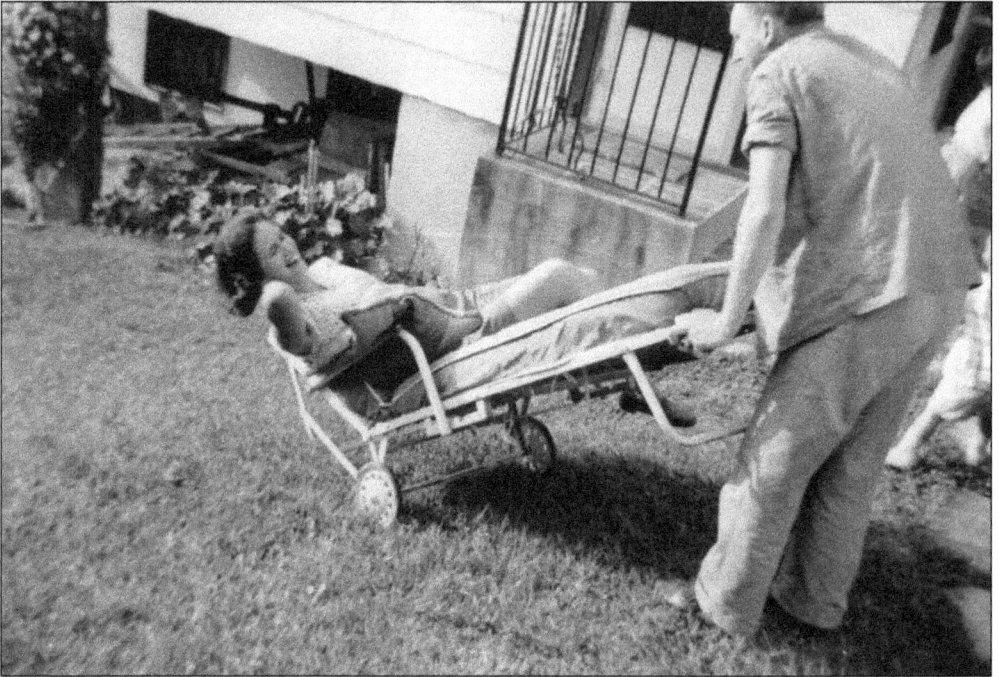

The author's parents are seen here before they were married. Catherine "K" Stevens and Bob Maher are having some playful fun during the summer. The author's grandmother only used the home as a summer residence. (Author's collection.)

Four

HOTELS AND BUSINESSES

Today, with Rockland Lake surrounded by the suburban building boom of the 1950s and 1960s, it is often hard to imagine back to a time when the lake was a tourist destination. However, it is because of the summer community that hotels and businesses were built—so many people from all over the New York metro area were visiting Rockland County. To this day, many Rockland County residents indicate that their families moved to the area after having visited the lake. Today, with most of the original hotels and businesses long gone, most visitors see Rockland Lake as a nice passive place to relax, not knowing it has not always been like that. Rockland Lake was a happening tourist location with casinos, bars, dance halls, and all forms of general recreation. An 1875 letter to the editor of the *Rockland County Journal* clearly expresses the attraction of the Lake. The following is an excerpt from that letter:

> Dear Sir, I do not lay any claim to philanthropy, but I should like to see your readers enjoy themselves, as they certainly must in Rockland County, where every blessing that nature can bestow is given them . . . The place I refer to is Rockland Lake, and the name I fear is too often associated in the imagination, with mammoth, ice-houses, heaps of saw dust, ice carts, wagons and all the other necessities of that business. The visitor there, will find that the ice-houses are quite picturesque in themselves. Their pure white exteriors forming a very agreeable contrast with the green hills in the background. But the clear, smooth water of the Lake, and its surrounding scenery, absorb the mind to such an extent, that all else is forgotten.

The letter goes on and is signed simply "A New Yorker." With write-ups like that in the newspaper, it is no wonder that Rockland Lake would require extensive hotels and businesses.

This 1960s picture is of the Congers Hotel, located on Route 9W and Congers Lake Road at the North entrance into Rockland Lake State Park. (Courtesy of the PIPC Archives.)

The Congers Hotel was also referred to as the Gin Bar. Signs promoting "cold beer to take out" were to entice the visitors to the park. (Courtesy of the PIPC Archives.)

This Esso gas station was located at the original north entrance into Rockland Lake before the PIPC did any road improvements in the park. (Courtesy of the PIPC Archives.)

The Alfred Sieglings Agency was for real estate and ticket agents. The round signs on the front of the building are of steamships. (Collection of Robert Knight.)

Rockland Lake Lodge, also known as "fishermen's home," was located where the present-day Rockland Lake fishing station is on the west side of the lake. One can see the icehouses in the background and the cove in the mountain ridge where the town sits and has access to the Hudson River. (Author's collection.)

This is a front view of the Rockland Lake Lodge, and the upper right of the postcard advertises dining and dancing as main attractions. (Author's collection.)

Here is Rockland Lake Lodge's dock. Fishermen and boats used the dock. (Author's collection.)

The Margard Hotel was considered one of the finer hotels at Rockland Lake. It was located toward the south end of the lake. (Collection of Robert Knight.)

Newcomb Inn, Rockland Lake, Rockland County, N. Y.

The Newcomb Inn was located near the south end of the lake. The inn earned a bit of fame after a federal court decision ordered the fence erected by former Sen. E.M. Rabenold between the road and Rockland Lake be taken down. Deputy O'Brien spent the night on the porch keeping an eye on the property to ensure Senator Rabenold did not reinstall the fence. (Collection of Robert Knight.)

The Windmill was located along Route 9W on the western side of the lake and offered "Tasty Home Cooking and Baking" in 1926. (Collection of Robert Knight.)

Harry Bartow's Blue Urn Restaurant, Rockland Lake, N. Y. Choice Liquors. Steaks and Sea Foods a Specialty. Clambakes and Barbecues. Telephones Rockland Lake 86 and 374

Harry Bartow's Blue Urn was a favorite among the locals for its fine food and good times. (Collection of Robert Knight)

Harry Bartow's BLUE URN
A Unique Bar and Grill
All Kinds of Good Food
Rockland Lake, N. Y.

Harry Bartow's Blue Urn also was known for its beer garden. Many a summer night, people from all over would enjoy the beer garden. (Collection of Robert Knight.)

This view of the Blue Urn shows a sign to the left of the building for Kramer's cabins. It was a family-oriented place to spend the summer. (Courtesy of the PIPC Archives.)

In this 1960s picture, from right to left, one sees the Blue Urn, a sign for Route 9W, Kramer's Cabins, a large traffic light, and the original south entrance into Rockland Lake. Today, the south entrance into the park runs right through where the Blue Urn was located. (Courtesy of the PIPC Archives.)

Here is the south entrance of the park in the 1960s. To the left is the Quaspeck Casino. In the closing car chase scenes of *BUtterfield* 8, starring Elizabeth Taylor, the Quaspeck Casino can be seen in the background. (Courtesy of the PIPC Archives.)

Exterior view of Quaspeck Casino, Rockland Lake N. Y.
Meals served at all hours Phone Congers 201.

"Meals [are] served at all hours," according to this advertisement for the Quaspeck Casino. The casino was an after-hours hot spot for town folk. (Author's collection.)

INTERIOR VIEW OF QUASPECK CASINO. ROCKLAND LAKE. N. Y.

Pictured is the inside of Quaspeck Casino. It offered a large dance floor and good food. This building was owned by Sen. E.M. Rabenold, who later sold the property to the state for the expansion of Rockland Lake State Park. (Collection of Robert Knight.)

Terrace at rear of Quaspeck Casino,
Rockland Lake N. Y.
Meals served year round. Parties
catered to. Phone Congers 201

The Quaspeck Casino was more than just a nightclub hot spot. By day, it was a family gathering place for lunch and a swim in the lake. (Collection of Robert Knight.)

Pavilion at rear of Quaspeck
Casino, Rockland Lake N. Y.
Dining and dancing at Casino.
Phone Congers 201.

The Quaspeck Casino's bathing pavilion and bathhouse was for swimmers at the lake. This picture is from the 1920s. (Collection of Robert Knight.)

Quaspeck Casino also provided entrainment to children. The club developed into a close community of regular families. (Collection of Robert Knight.)

Quaspeck Casino is seen in this 1920s aerial view. In 1958, when Sen. E.M. Rabenold sold the club to the PIPC, a number of improvements were made. However, by the late 1960s, after the opening of the new North Rockland Lake State Park Pool complex, these buildings were removed to make way for a new south pool that opened in the 1970s. (Collection of Robert Knight.)

The Bobin was a notorious night spot on 9W just south of the park. It was known for its first-class jazz musicians who would travel up from New York City to play all night to a full house. (Collection of Robert Knight.)

Bobin Country Club
"21 Miles North of Geo. Washington Bridge"
On Rt. 9W, Rockland Lake, N. Y.

The Bobin also had cabins for summer rentals. Part of the attractions were a handball court and table tennis. (Collection of Robert Knight.)

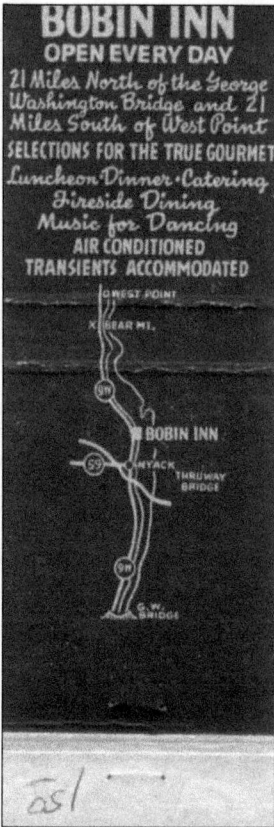

BOBIN INN
OPEN EVERY DAY
21 Miles North of the George
Washington Bridge and 21
Miles South of West Point
SELECTIONS FOR THE TRUE GOURMET
Luncheon·Dinner·Catering
Fireside Dining
Music for Dancing
AIR CONDITIONED
TRANSIENTS ACCOMMODATED

This matchbook cover shows the funky spirit of the Bobin, advertising such luxuries as central heat and air-conditioning. It is interesting to note that the inside of this matchbook cover stated, "Transients Accommodated," as in later years, during the 1970s and the 1980s, before the building was closed, it had become a seedy night spot. (Author's collection.)

JOHNNY'S WONDER BAR,
ROUTE 9-W, CONGERS, N.Y.
TEL. CONGERS - 961

Jonny's Wonder Bar was another happening night spot for the local and summer crowds that stayed at Rockland Lake. This was the era of big bands and jazz. (Collection of Robert Knight.)

The Cozzi Bungalow Colony houses are still located on 9W south of the park entrance. These bungalows are now year-round residences. (Author's collection.)

Shown is the entrance to Camp Ha-Ya, at Pine Grove, Rockland Lake. The number of camps and bungalows show just how popular a tourist destination Rockland Lake was prior to the 1960s. (Collection of Robert Knight.)

3-9   The Cottages, Ha-Ya Camp, Pine Grave at Rockland Lake, N. Y.

Camp Ha-Ya cottages are seen here; this camp is no longer in existence. (Collection of Robert Knight.)

The Floridian Cottages at Rockland Lake had a pool and casino. It offered entertainment for the whole family with its day camp. (Courtesy of the PIPC Archives.)

The Applebaum's Modern Cottages. This 1960s picture does not show the better side of what once was a thriving summer community. By the time the PIPC was buying Rockland Lake and the sounding land that people were willing to sell, it was the end of the summer cottage rental business. With better roads to New York City, city people were now just making day trips to enjoy the lake. Most cottages and bungalow communities were pleased to sell, as their businesses were coming to an end. (Courtesy of the PIPC Archives.)

Five

CAMPS

Camping at Hook Mountain and Rockland Lake was a big yearly experience for so many families and young boys and girls from New York City. One of the first organized camps at Rockland Lake was Camp John Pershing. The Junior Training Camp Association of New York City established this camp in 1915 after an outbreak of trachoma had developed in Lower East Side schools. In a 1918 brochure, the camp indicates that West Point cadets did instruction and direction and that the cost was $1 per day. Later, former ambassador to Germany James W. Gerard, who owned a lodge on the top of Hook Mountain, established a camp. In a radio broadcast on May 5, 1934, Gerard, in commenting on the Communist May Day Parade, said, "Most of the participants were young and the Communists maintained summer camps for boys' and girls." This was his reason to form his own boys' and girls' camps. More than 300 boys and girls attended his free, one-month summer camp. Today, despite the still beautiful location of Hook Mountain and Rockland Lake, camping is no longer permitted.

Seen at Camp John Pershing (named for General Pershing) in 1914, Boy Scouts of America Troop No. 111 of the Bedford YMCA enjoys camping on the banks of the Hudson River after the rock quarry operations closed. (Courtesy of the PIPC Archives.)

Camp John Pershing was run by the Junior Training Camp Association in New York City. Here, it advertises "Real Military Training for Boys with instruction by West Point Cadets, Third year class." Note the Palisades cliffs in the background. (Courtesy of the PIPC Archives.)

This is a view of Camp John Pershing from the Hudson River with tents by the shoreline. The camp offered instruction in field fortifications, military engineering, athletics, and bridge and road building. (Courtesy of the PIPC Archives.)

Campus — Camp Gerard for Boys, Rockland Lake, N. Y.

After the PIPC established Hook Mountain State Park, Camp John Pershing tents and buildings became Camp Gerard. (Collection of Robert Knight.)

Pictured is the Hook Mountain police camping check-in station in the 1900s. (Courtesy of the PIPC Archives.)

Athletic Field — Camp Gerard for Boys, Rockland Lake, N. Y.

This is an aerial view of Camp Gerard's athletic field and the former Camp John Pershing parade grounds. (Collection of Robert Knight)

Camp Gerard also had a separate camp for girls at Rockland Lake. The mess hall was accessed by the La Tour Bridge. (Collection of Robert Knight.)

Camp John Pershing general store and mess hall are seen here. The sign to the left reads, "Camp John Pershing, Rockland Lake, Congers Branch of the American Red Cross." The small sign on the left by the open stand reads, "We Sell Schmitts Ice Cream." This building was located by Rockland Lake. (Courtesy of the PIPC Archives.)

These men are some of the West Point cadets who provided instruction to the boys attending Camp John Pershing. (Courtesy of the PIPC Archives.)

The cost of the Camp John Pershing field tents was a dollar a day with everything included. It was offered to boys who had little means to escape the New York City summer heat. At camp, they learned basic military training. An advertising tagline was "Fit yourself for your Country's service during your vacation." (Courtesy of the PIPC Archives.)

THE LOG CABIN on top of MOUNTAIN, ROCKLAND LAKE, N.Y.

Rockland Lake also had cabins for people to spend their summer vacations. (Author's collection.)

Camp life at Hook Mountain is seen in the 1900s. Even the little boy sitting by the tent in the background is wearing a tie. (Author's collection.)

Camp Eramer, Congers, Rockland Lake, N.Y.

Camp Eramer was named after a family. Times have changed since the 1900s; note the man camping in a tie and jacket. A woman is seen washing dishes in the background. Only the dog truly seems to be enjoying the trip. (Author's collection.)

We all love the
Soldier Boys at

Rockland Lake,
N. Y.

Don't miss it
It's Great.

"We all love the soldier boys at Rockland Lake"; the men here are most likely cadets from West Point, working at Camp John Pershing around the time of World War I. This postcard would have been considered a bit on the provocative side during this time. (Author's collection.)

Six

EARLY PARKS AND RECREATION

Rockland Lake has always been a place of contradictions and attractions. As the only natural lake in Rockland County formed by springs, the local Lenni-Lenape tribe, who called the lake "Quashpeak," understood its importance as a clear water pond. The early English settlers enjoyed its abundance of freshwater fish, and the ever expanding New York City population only 30 miles away saw its great potential to provide ice to maintain and store the city's growing food demands. However, the lake was much more than a natural resource to be used for profit. The location of the lake is encircled on three sides by the Palisades cliffs, giving a perfect background for some of the most beautiful Hudson Valley vistas. It is the lake's natural setting that drew people every week from New York City and around the world to enjoy its beauty. The early park and recreation use of the lake predates the development of the Nyack Beach and Hook Mountain State Parks, which were only formed in the 1910s. It is interesting to note that, once the Nyack Beach and Hook Mountain parks were established, most people visited them by steamboat and would not make the climb up the hill into the town of Rockland Lake or visit the lake itself. The Hudson River parks and Rockland Lake could have been miles away. The fact that so many industrial and recreational activities occurred in such a small area is one of Rockland Lake's main contradictions.

No. 7, Rockland Lake, N. Y. (Barker's Cove.)

11 ~   27 ~   '05

Barker's Cove was a guest resort and lodge along the north side of Rockland Lake. It was located where the current north pool building of Rockland Lake State Park is today. (Author's collection.)

Barker's Cove rowboats are lined up and waiting for the summertime crowds. Rockland Lake remains a noted fishing spot. (Courtesy of the PIPC Archives.)

This Barker's Cove postcard is announcing the Knickerbocker-Turnverein games to be held at Rockland Lake Park on Sunday, July 14, 1907. The Turnverein was an association of gymnasts founded in 1811 in Germany. Shown are some of the attractions, including a shooting gallery, gambling tables, boat races, swimming, and drinking. All guests arrived via a special West Shore train from New York City. (Courtesy of Robert Knight.)

ROCKLAND LAKE AT VALLEY COTTAGE, N. Y.

Four young girls are enjoying the water at the edge of the lake. (Courtesy of Robert Knight.)

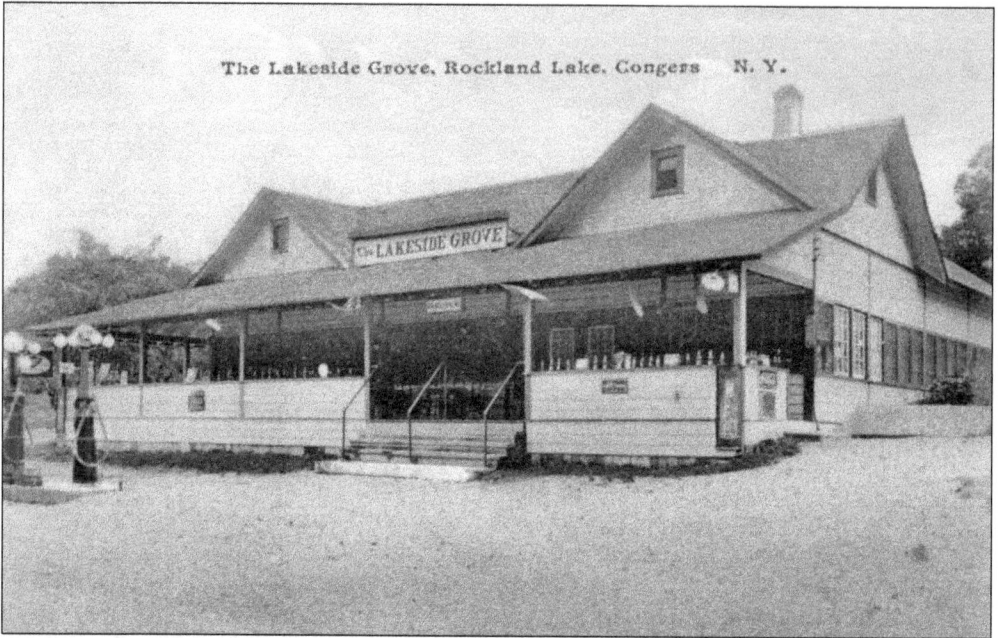

The Lakeside Grove, Rockland Lake, Congers N. Y.

The Lake Side Grove, located on the north side of the lake, had something for everyone. By day, it was the place to grab a cold coke and sandwich while filling up one's car with gas. It was also a place to relax and go for a swim in the lake behind the building. (Courtesy of Robert Knight.)

Interior of The Lakeside Grove, Rockland Lake, Congers N. Y.

The interior of the Lake Side Grove was a large dance hall for nighttime entertainment and live bands. (Courtesy of Robert Knight.)

Sylvan Grove was one of the first lakeside amusement areas and boat docks for the public to use at the lake. (Author's collection.)

Sylvan Grove was one of the main picnic areas around Rockland Lake. It was often the spot for many church gatherings and the annual picnic of the Rockland County Farmers Club. (Author's collection.)

Sylvan Grove was located at the present-day Rockland Lake State Park's Nature Center. This area was also the terminus of the Rockland Lake-to-Congers train, making Sylvan Grove an easy train ride from New York City. (Author's collection.)

The same crystal-clear, spring-fed waters that gave the Rockland Lake ice its worldwide reputation also allowed for great enjoyment in the form of swimming during the summer months. (Courtesy of Robert Knight.)

Amusements at Rockland Lake were many. Here is a typical strongman or high striker game. The caption in the upper right reads, "Striking for a raise at Old Bill Thompson's Striker." The first lower sign on the pole reads, "Ladies Average." (Courtesy of Robert Knight.)

OLD BILL THOMPSON'S BABY GAME AT ROCKLAND LAKE PARK, N. Y.

This is "Old Bill Thompson's Baby Game," where one could get three balls for 5¢. (Author's collection.)

THOMPSON'S SOUVENIR BUILDING, ROCKLAND LAKE PARK, N. Y.

Here is Thompson's souvenir stand. Candy, tobacco, and cigars as well as other items were sold here. (Author's collection.)

Here is a group of young children playing ball at one of the many fields around Rockland Lake. (Courtesy of Robert Knight.)

The amusements continued late into the night, adding to the reputation of all Rockland Lake had to offer New York City residents who were trying to escape the city heat. (Author's collection.)

This postcard's caption reads, "Lovers at Rockland Lake, N.Y." Even today, many lovers find Rockland Lake to be the perfect place for marriage proposals and weddings. The allure of Rockland Lake can best be expressed by a poem written by Willie F. Gilchrest of Brooklyn and published in the *Rockland County Journal* on April 7, 1862, "Calm, beautiful lake what joy I feel, As swiftly I glide across thy stream, And gayly ply my oar, What pleasant hours on thee I have passed, Viewing thy lovely shore. Years may pass ere I see thee again, Perhaps my heart will be filled with pain, I'll love thee but the more." (Author's collection.)

Seven

FORMATION OF
CURRENT PARKS

In a 100-year span, no other New York City metropolitan area has evolved as much as Rockland Lake. Since the 1830s, when the first ice was cut and shipped to New York City, Rockland Lake has been the "icebox of the city." In the late 1920s, when the ice industry closed, Rockland Lake evolved into a tourist destination to spend summer days. The Palisades Interstate Park Commission recognized the importance and the attractiveness this area had to offer. Since the early Nyack Beach and Hook Mountain State Parks in the 1920s, it was always a goal to make the area into a grander summer getaway. Over the years, many plans were made to realize this dream. It was not until 1958, when former Sen. E.M. Rabenold sold to the PIPC the 256-acre lake and the 225 acres of surrounding land, that the dream of the PIPC for a grand summer getaway became a reality. During the summer of 1958, the PIPC sent out letters to all of the property owners in Rockland Lake asking if they may be interested in selling their property. By the end of 1959, the PIPC had purchased a total of 771 acres of the town of Rockland Lake. To this day, there are still negative feelings from some of the original residents, as they felt they had to sell their homes to the PIPC; however, land condemnation was never put into practice. By 1959, the residents had grown up with the PIPC as their neighbor for the past 50 years with the development of the River Parks. By the early 1960s, the town of Rockland Lake disappeared, and the new north pool complex was opened in June 1965, which officially opened Rockland Lake State Park. The south pool complex was opened in 1969, allowing the park to accommodate 25,000 to 30,000 people per day.

This model shows that, in the 1920s, with the development of Hook Mountain State Park (Hook Mountain is on the left), a plan was considered to acquire all of the town of Rockland Lake and flatten out the mountain between the lake and the river. Keeping in mind that the lake sits 168 feet above the river, there would still be a sizeable elevation change from the lake to the river's edge. A ball field and track were to be constructed, as seen in the center of the model. The

money to cover the cost of this project was to come from the continued sale of the traprock, as most of Hook Mountain and the mountain between the lake and river were removed. It was also suggested at this time that a road be built from Upper Nyack along the river's edge to Haverstraw. (Courtesy of the PIPC Archives.)

This 1950 plan for the development of Hook Mountain State Park shows a pool and bathhouses at the base of Hook Mountain. (Courtesy of the PIPC Archives.)

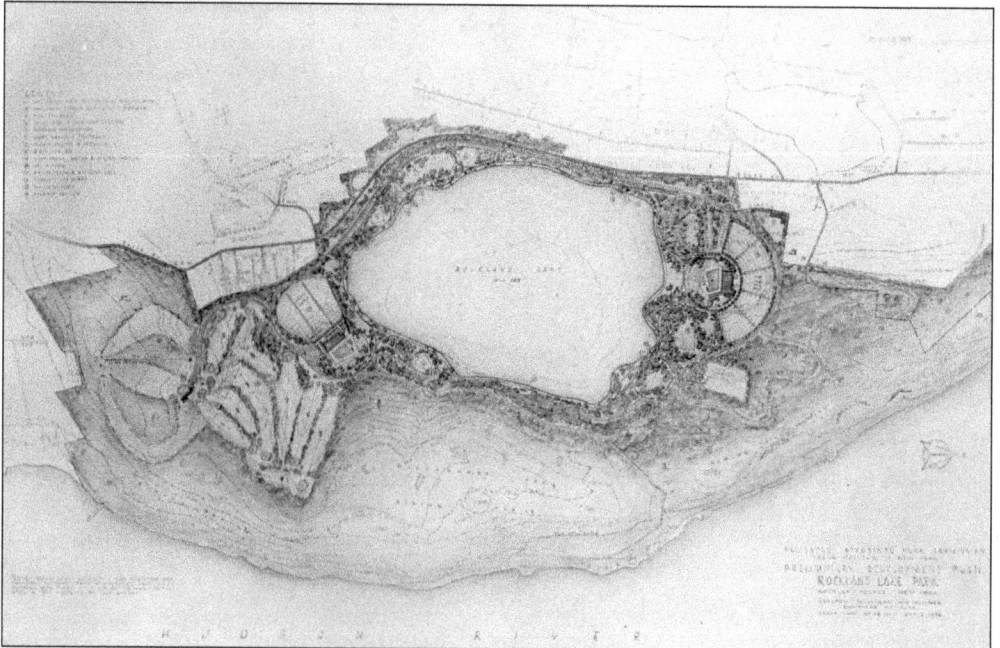

This 1958 plan for the development of Rockland Lake shows the town of Rockland Lake completely removed and the park developing the area of the former town. (Courtesy of the PIPC Archives.)

This aerial view is of the north entrance into Rockland Lake. The Hudson River is on the top left, and Rockland Lake is on the right. The town is in the center with most of its buildings still standing. The original Lake Road ran through what is present-day parking lot No. 1 for the north pool complex. (Courtesy of the PIPC Archives.)

This is an aerial view of the south entrance into Rockland Lake, with the Quaspeck Casino lakeside. Hudson River is seen at the top of the photograph. (Courtesy of the PIPC Archives.)

Here is the opening-day journal for the Rockland Lake State Park North Pool Complex. The complex was designed to handle 15,000 people a day. (Courtesy of the PIPC Archives.)

School buses are unloading for the north pool. The author remembers as a child trying to count as many as 300 buses on any given weekend in the parking lot. (Courtesy of the PIPC Archives.)

Pictured in 1965, Gov. Nelson Rockefeller (second from the left) is eating lunch opening day at the north pool complex. Much of the funding for the development of Nyack Beach, Hook Mountain, and Rockland Lake State Parks came from the Rockefeller foundation. (Courtesy of the PIPC Archives.)

Gov. Nelson Rockefeller (center) is talking with other invited guests on opening day. (Courtesy of the PIPC Archives.)

Gov. Nelson Rockefeller is signing autographs for the guest at opening day of the North Pool complex. (Courtesy of the PIPC Archives.)

A group of eager children waits to get back into the pool for another swim on opening day. (Courtesy of the PIPC Archives.)

The Rockland Lake pool was one of the largest public pools constructed in the state at this time. It offered diving and a kiddy pool for toddlers. (Courtesy of the PIPC Archives.)

The 60th anniversary Boy Scout Jamboree was held at Rockland Lake in 1970. (Courtesy of the PIPC Archives.)

The Cairngorn bagpipe and drum club from New City, New York, attended the Boy Scout Jamboree. (Courtesy of the PIPC Archives.)

The 60th anniversary Boy Scout Jamboree was full of events. (Courtesy of the PIPC Archives.)

The Rockland County Model Airplane Club held yearly events at Rockland Lake. (Courtesy of the PIPC Archives.)

The construction of the nature trail and zoo is seen on the former site of Sylvan Grove. (Courtesy of the PIPC Archives.)

In 1965, the Rockland Lake State Park Nature Center and Zoo were favorite attractions. However, following the economic downturn of the 1970s, the nature center and zoo closed. Since the fall of 2008, work has been underway to revitalize the nature center and the surrounding trail with the great help of many volunteers. (Courtesy of the PIPC Archives.)

Throughout the years, Rockland Lake, Hook Mountain, and Nyack Beach have offered so much to so many—from one of the world's best-known ice-harvesting operations and rock quarries that help build New York City to endless summers of relaxing vacations around the lake. This 1960s image of people ice sailing depicts another adventure the area has to offer. Today, watching the local sculling clubs practice rowing on the lake is testimony that the area continues to serve a diverse community. (Courtesy of the PIPC Archives.)

BIBLIOGRAPHY

The Story of Hook Mountain. Booklet. New York, 1906.

Cole, David, DD, ed. *History of Rockland County, New York.* NY: J.B. Beers & Co., 1884.

Dobbin, William J. "Rockland Lake." *South of the Mountains* 7.3 (July–September, 1963).

Fact sheet: Ice Cutting at Rockland Lake. Rockland Lake Program Center.

Green, Frank Bertangue, MD. *The History of Rockland County.* NY: A.S. Barnes & Co., 1886.

Ice Harvesting Industry, Rockland Lake, N.Y. Rockland Lake Program Center.

Stott, Peter. "The Knickerbocker Ice Company and Inclined Railway at Rockland Lake, New York." *The Journal of the Society for Industrial Archeology* 5.1 (1979).

Visit us at
arcadiapublishing.com

www.ingramcontent.com/pod-product-compliance
Lightning Source LLC
Chambersburg PA
CBHW050659150426

42813CB00055B/2270